CHOICES

A CHRISTMAS SERVICE AND PAGEANT FOR THE ENTIRE CONGREGATION

J. B. QUISENBERRY

C.S.S. Publishing Co., Inc.

Lima, Ohio

CHOICES

9046 / ISBN 1-55673-258-9   PRINTED IN U.S.A.

Production Notes

This service is designed to involve a large number of children from the age of three years through High School. Very young children may be used as both shepherds and angels, as long as there are older angels and shepherds to guide them. Mary, Joseph, the Inn Keeper, and his Wife are best played by fifth or sixth graders. The readers and the characters should come from the Jr. High and High School classes. They may present their parts either as dramatic readings or memorized monologs, with or without special costumes. The beginning skit should be done by two fifth, sixth, or seventh graders as the children, and two High School students as the parents. The leader may be either an adult or a High School student.

The sets should be kept very simple. The costumes may range from bath robes to authentic period clothing.

The production time is about fifty minutes.

Choices

Prelude

Opening Skit

> *(The setting is a modern living room with the Father work-ing at a small table to the right and two children playing on the floor center stage. The choir enters singing a traditional Christmas Hymn and wearing hats and scarves to suggest outer wear. They proceed toward the left side of the altar area. A door bell rings, and the oldest child crosses down left and pantomimes opening a door.)*

Oldest Child: Look! Christmas carolers! *(The other child runs to door.)* Dad, come quick! There are carolers at the door!

Father: That's nice. *(He does not look up from his work.)*

Younger Child: Dad, hurry up! You'll miss them!

Father: I don't have time right now. I've got to finish this report. You can tell me about it later.

Younger Child: *(He runs right and calls offstage.)* Mom! There are carolers outside! Come and see them!

Mother: *(from offstage)* I'll be there in a minute, Honey. I've got to get these cookies into the oven or you won't have any for your party at school tomorrow.

(The choir stops singing and exits to the choir loft. The children close the door and go back to their places on the floor.)

Mother: *(enters from the right)* The cookies are all ready for tomorrow. I thought you said that there were carolers at the door.

Oldest Child: We did.

Younger Child: They were great!

Oldest Child: It was really neat! You missed it, Mom.

(Lights out, spotlight on choir. During the black out the set should be changed to a stable.)

Welcome
Leader: Welcome to you, and peace to you all! We come together today in celebration and remembrance of that most blessed night so many years ago, when the stillness of the winter sky was pierced by a baby's first cry. In what better way can we remember that night than through the actions of our own children? As the prophet said, "a little child shall lead them." So come with us now to that holy night when the miracle of birth was visited upon a young couple from

Nazareth and the miracle of salvation came to all people in the form of a tiny baby. Come and wonder with the shepherds at that most wonderful event — the birth of Christ!

Choral Anthem "O Come, O Come, Emmanuel"
(During the anthem, choir members will read the following verses from Isaiah, one after each of the first, second, and third verses.)

1. Isaiah 7:14. "Therefore the Lord Himself shall give you a sign; Behold a virgin shall conceive, and bear a son, and shall call his name Immanuel."

2. Isaiah 9:2. "The people that walked in darkness have seen a great light; they that dwell in the land of the shadow of death, upon them hath the light shined."

3. Isaiah 9:6. "For unto us a child is born, unto us a son is given: and the government shall be upon his shoulder: and his name shall be called Wonderful, Counsellor, The Mighty God, The Everlasting Father, The Prince of Peace."

The Pageant *(lights on manger)*

First Reader: When Caesar Augustus made his tax decree, it was a hardship for many. The roads were filled with people going to be counted and taxed in the cities of their ancestors.

Among this throng, there was a couple from Nazareth. There was nothing unusual about them, just a carpenter and his wife, expecting their first child. Thousands must have passed them on the road to Bethlehem without a second glance. And yet, the baby that would be born to this couple would change the world forever.

A Wealthy Woman: There were so many people on the road that day! All of us were in a hurry. You see, it was obvious to everyone that it would be difficult to find a place to stay in the City of David. Bethlehem didn't have nearly enough inns to accommodate so many people.

Of course I wasn't as worried as some. I was sure to get there ahead of the crowd. My team of horses would see to that. I could travel much faster than most of the people, who were on foot. Besides, I was sure to find a room, even if I arrived in the city of my ancestors late. Money speaks loudly, you see. I knew that many of my fellow travelers would not be so fortunate.

I almost stopped and offered one couple a ride. They looked so tired, and the young woman was great with child. But you have to be careful, you know. You can never tell about strangers, no matter how innocent they look. Why, they may have been thieves! Besides, I wanted to get to my destination as soon as possible. I didn't want to have to settle for a room below my station. So I left them there on the road. I'm sure they made it to Bethlehem eventually.

Second Reader: *(Mary and Joseph enter at back of church)* By the time Mary and Joseph reached Bethlehem, they were hungry, dusty, tired, and in desperate need of a place to stay. The streets were clogged with people. Vainly, they went from inn to inn in search of a bed and a meal. Mary kept up a good front, but Joseph could see the strain in her eyes. She was due to have the baby any day now; he had to find a place for her to rest! Joseph's worry grew to near panic as inn keeper after inn keeper informed them that there was no room available. *(As Mary and Joseph approach the front of the church, the Inn Keeper and his wife meet them at the center of the communion rail.)* Joseph had almost given up when they came to an inn on the edge of town. The inn keeper repeated the phrase that Joseph had heard so many times — "No Room."

(Mary and Joseph and the Inn Keeper and his wife should pantomime the conversation as the reader continues.)

The usually quiet carpenter could not stand any more. Mary hadn't complained, but he could see how tired she was.

"There must be something!" he argued, "My wife is expecting, and the journey has been so hard on her!"

The inn keeper's wife could see that Mary's time was near. She could see how uncomfortable she was. "What about the stable?" she asked her husband. "It's not much, but it is clean and warm."

Joseph readily agreed. The inn keeper's wife gave them some blankets, and her husband showed Mary and Joseph to the stable.

(The Inn Keeper leads Mary and Joseph to the manger which should be situated centrally, near the altar, and then leaves. Joseph should place a blanket around Mary's shoulders as she kneels on one side of the manger, then he should kneel at the other side.)

Inn Keeper: That was quite a time! Thanks to Caesar's census, all of Judea was on the move, and in need of a place to stay. I wonder if Caesar knew what a big favor he did for us inn keepers. We had people sleeping three and four to a bed! All of them paid full price, too!

I don't know if I saw Mary and Joseph from Nazareth or not. There were so many people that we had to turn away. Their faces all melt together, if you know what I mean. Believe me, if I could have squeezed them in, I would have. I never turn my back on money if I can avoid it. But we did turn a lot of people away in the days of census. I hated to do it, but we had no choice. You can only fit so many people into one building.

9

I may have seen the young couple from Nazareth; I don't know. Like I said, after a while they all look the same to me.

Music *(soprano or alto solo)*   "Sweet Little Jesus Boy"

Third Reader: *(Mary takes the baby from hiding and cuddles it, and lays it in the manger.)* Later that night, the silence of the Judean plain was pierced by a baby's first cry. The Son of God, the Savior of all humankind, was lovingly and tenderly wrapped in swaddling cloths and laid in a manger.

Joseph looked down with wonder at his new foster child. Would he be up to the great task that God had given him? He was only a simple carpenter. What if he made mistakes raising God's Son?

But Mary's heart was at peace. It was a peace that she had known since the angel had spoken to her nine months before. Her face glowed with love as she looked down at her sleeping son, and then up into her husband's eyes.

Music *(soprano or alto solo)*   "Ave Maria"

(During the song, the shepherds enter from the back of the sanctuary and proceed up the center aisle to the communion rail, where they pantomine with the angels as their story is read.)

Fourth Reader: As Mary and Joseph shared that holy silence, shepherds, watching over their flocks, were startled by a bright light *(Enter Angels from the right)* and a voice from heaven. They covered their faces and shook with fear. But the voice was gentle.

"Don't be afraid," it said.

10

The shepherds looked up and saw an angel in white robes standing in front of them. And just beyond, a host of angels sang God's praises to the sky.

"I bring you good tidings of great joy, which shall be to all people," the angel said. "For unto you is born this day, in the City of David, a Savior, which is Christ the Lord. And this shall be a sign unto you; you shall find the babe wrapped in swaddling cloths, and lying in a manger." Then all the angels joined in singing, "Glory to God in the highest, and on earth, peace, and good will toward all men!" *(The angels exit to stand behind the manger. Shepherds kneel in front of manger.)*

Fifth Reader: When the angels had ascended, the shepherds left their flocks and hurried to the stable on the outskirts of Bethlehem. When they got there, they saw Mary and Joseph, and the baby sleeping in the manger, just as the angels had said that they would. This was not the way they had expected the Messiah to come to them. The surroundings were humble, but they fell on their knees at the sight of him, and worshiped their newborn King.

Later, three kings from the East would do the same, but on that holiest of nights, it was a few simple shepherds that God chose to witness the greatest event of all time: the birth of Jesus Christ.

(The Readers and all the other children with the exception of Mary, Jospeh, and the shepherds, who maintain their positions, join the angels to form a half circle behind the manger.)

Music *all participating children*   "Away in the Manger"

(After the song, all the children except Mary and Joseph may exit right. Mary and Joseph should maintain their positions on either side of the manger.)

Sixth Reader: The pageant is completed. You see before you the same sight that greeted the shepherds so many years ago: the stable, the manger, the young woman Mary — her face aglow with the special warmth that all new mothers know — Joseph beside her — happy beyond words — and finally the baby, so small, so helpless, lying in a manger.

We are not as lowly as the shepherds, nor as mighty as the kings who bowed low before this tiny child, but we, too, have heard the good news of the angels. We, too, are called upon to put off our worldly pride and kneel in true repentant humility before our infant Savior, singing prayers of thanksgiving, and filled with wonder at the great love our God bears us, that he would sacrifice his only Son for our salvation!

Leader: Come forward now and offer your gifts unto the Lord. *(At this point the ushers direct the congregation to place their offerings in baskets that are placed on the floor, in front of the manger. Holy Communion may also be administered at this time as the people kneel before the manger.)*

Offertory *(choir)*   "Oh Come All Ye Faithful"

(After all the people have returned to their seats, Mary and Joseph exit.)

Prayer *(in unison)*

Dear Lord, who gave your only Son for our Salvation, fill our hearts with the simple, steadfast love of a child. Keep the spirit of Christmas forever young in our hearts, so that, like shepherds, we may never cease to wonder at Thy love. Help us, Father, to come to you today, and enter into the boundless joy that the shepherds felt on that holiest of nights.

In the name of him whose birth we remember today, cleanse our souls, so that we might become as little children. And, like the Wise Men, help us to follow your star in our lives forever.

In the name of the Father, and of the Son, and of the Holy Spirit we pray. Amen

Music *(choir)* "Hark the Herald Angels Sing"

Seventh Reader: According to the Gospel, the shepherds, after they had worshiped their infant Savior, "made known abroad the saying which was told them concerning the child." What a wide variety of responses they must have received to the angel's story! There were many, undoubtedly, who believed and flocked to the stable to worship the King, and to share the joy that the shepherds had received. But there were others who, like so many people today, rejected the Good News, and were unable to share that joy.

Merchant: The shepherds? Yes, I heard their story, and the stories of others who visited the stable on the edge of town. I'm told that there were even three kings from the East who visited the young couple from Nazareth and their infant son. But the whole thing is just too fantastic to believe! The Son of God born in a stable? Surely, if God were to send his Son to earth in the form of a baby, he would be born to a king or a priest, not a carpenter, and especially not one from Nazareth of all places! I simply cannot believe that this child lying in a manger was the Son of the Almighty God.

Not that I wasn't curious. The child must have been remarkable, since so many who did go to see him came away believing that he was the Messiah. Oh yes, I was curious, but not curious enough to go to that dirty stable myself. I mean, what if the word got out that I, a respected member of the community, listened to the rantings of a bunch of star-struck shepherds?

No, I didn't go to see him. It wasn't worth the risk. A man's reputation is precious. I wasn't about to risk mine on the basis of such a fantastic tale. Angels talking to shepherds! A king born in a stable! Ridiculous!

Eighth Reader: And so it began on that holy night so long ago. A baby was born in a stable, a baby that thirty-three short years later would suffer the pain and humiliation of death on a Cross to offer us the gift of Salvation.

The story is fantastic. It seems inconceivable that one small child could have such power. But it is even more fantastic that God loves us so much that he would give his only Son as a sacrifice for our sin.

The choice is ours now. Do we walk comfortably away, wrapped in the security of intellect and propriety? Or do we, like the shepherds, throw off the things of this world, and embrace our Lord, our King, our Savior, Jesus Christ? Choose now. Choose life. Choose Christ! Come share the joy by joining us in song!

Congregational Hymn "Joy to the World"

Benediction

Postlude

www.ingramcontent.com/pod-product-compliance
Lightning Source LLC
Chambersburg PA
CBHW060045040426
42331CB00032B/2491